The Empathic Parent's Guide to Raising a Highly Sensitive Child

Parenting Strategies I Learned to
Understand and Nurture My Child's Gift

Freeda Meighan

Join Our Support Group

Finding a supportive community can be hard. Many parents feel like they are alone in their parenting struggles and that no one understands what it is like to raise children today. In order to make the most of your time and get more out of this book, I highly encourage you to join our active community on Facebook.

Don't be afraid to reach out. You're never alone in this journey, and these are excellent resources that can support you.

See you there,

Freeda Meighan

JOIN NOW

https://bit.ly/3zulOsI

Contents

Introduction

When Heather was growing up, I knew she was more special than other children. She was my eldest, and for a time, an only child. Since she was small, Heather was already a quiet child. I always thought she was mature for her age because instead of playing with other children, she was quite content sitting on her own, busy scribbling away with her crayons on a drawing board. We could even leave her alone for hours and she wouldn't mind. She was also very peculiar with noise. Whenever we would pass a mall with a blasting stereo, she would cover her eyes and cry. Heather would only calm down when we were back in the car, with a soothing lullaby in the background.

Heather was always particular about everything. I was quite exhausted at first because she had a lot of demands. She cannot eat orange foods or beans. She hated synthetic fiber and had allergic reactions when she wore wooly clothes. She had to be picked up at 4 PM after class or she'd fly into a rage. I was quite lost and angry at times because Heather would have tantrums and meltdowns in public when she didn't like something. From pleading to outright scolding, I tried to discipline Heather in the best way I could.

In my desperation, I sought the advice of a friend on what to do. She was a mother of my daughter's classmate and she could empathize with my dilemma. Her son was also very picky, and she was as lost as I was. But my friend told me to read about the "Highly Sensitive Person," a trait that she thought fitted my daughter very much. There were not a lot of resources, but I tried to read as many books and internet sources as I could. The more I read about highly sensitive persons, the more I felt that I understood Heather more.

From being insecure and lost about taking care of Heather, I began to see her more as a gift I needed to take care of. I began to accept Heather for who she is, an emotional and precocious kid who needed my help more than ever. I began to tolerate some of her eccentricities and particular needs but also made sure I didn't spoil her. In turn, I saw that Heather began to open up to me. From being a recluse and quiet child, she began to confide in me her little secrets and thoughts. In her little ways, she found ways to surprise me with her thoughtfulness. She still had her tantrums, but I was able to set definite rules, so she didn't have her way all the time. It was like cultivating a rare flower that slowly bloomed into beauty.

This book is an account of my journey with Heather. I now have two other kids and I have tried to treat them with the same love as I have for Heather. The insights in this book come from my personal experience of taking care of a highly sensitive child. I had a lot of errors along the way, but these errors proved valuable in teaching me lessons. Until now, I am learning a lot from taking care of Heather and I feel very happy seeing her grow before my eyes. I want to impart my knowledge on highly sensitive persons in the hope that more parents can readily identify the trait in their children and make the necessary steps in order to change the way they approach their children. Left to unguided hands, highly sensitive children can deteriorate, closing doors of communication and hiding in their shells. I want to build communities of care so that our gifted children will always feel that they are loved especially for their unique gifts. This book wishes to end the stigma against HSCs and what we can do for our children who may be gifted with sensitivity.

Chapter 1

Understanding the Gift

What is a Highly Sensitive Person (HSP)? One of the pioneers in understanding the trait of highly sensitive persons is Dr. Elaine Aron. She conducted research and came out with a book called "The Highly Sensitive Person," outlining the characteristics of these types of people. Through her extensive research, Dr. Aron was able to help a lot of people in understanding themselves with this common and yet not too discussed personality trait of being sensitive. Her work has spawned other research as many people began to be more curious about the topic and how people with this condition can be approached.

In terms of prevalence, Dr. Aron says that around 15-20% of the population is considered "highly sensitive." With a substantial percentage, HSPs are considered normal though not prevalent. This is important to note because the usual understanding of HSP is that being too sensitive is a disease or disorder that must be cured and be rid of. People who are highly sensitive may be seen as "too shy," "high maintenance," "too picky," or just unreasonably sensitive. Management of HSPs has been directed to a medical approach, as if being too sensitive can go away with a few pills. This is a gross misunderstanding of what being an HSP is. A reductive and narrow kind of thinking like this may hurt HSPs in the short and long run. They are a normal part of our population even though they may not fit the more popular or usual personality traits we know of.

An HSP is someone who has a heightened sense of their surroundings, who displays strong reactivity to internal and external stimuli, who has increased emotional connectedness and who has a predisposition to turn inwards. This definition may be difficult to understand but we can unpack these traits one by one. Bear in mind people you may know who have this or observe your children if you feel that they display some of these behaviors.

HSPs pay close attention to internal and external stimuli. These people have sensory receptors which are able to pick up much more sensation than normal people. This does not refer to any anatomical excess. HSPs are not people with more eyes, more noses, more ears, or more receptors in their skin than the normal population. Rather, these people have receptors that are more sensitive to stimuli. Their senses are heightened more than most people. For example, HSPs can be very particular to the smell of their surroundings. If normal people go to a room without noticing anything, HSPs may pick up certain smells that may not be apparent.

In terms of touch, HSPs can be very particular to skin sensations. In terms of clothing, some even develop hypersensitive reactions to certain kinds of fabrics. They can be very picky in what kind of clothes they wear because the clothes would be stimulating their body the whole time they are worn. Touch also includes temperature. HSPs are more sensitive to temperature changes, either feeling too cold or too hot when the rest may not complain. The reaction may be manifested dermatologically at times. Still on the subject of touch, HSPs can also be more sensitive to movement. They may be more alert when there is sudden movement near them, like when a ball comes directly at them, or a person suddenly hugs them from behind. They are filled with a rush of adrenaline as though they are being attacked. They can also react too readily, running away at the slightest movement or moving to a defensive position. They do not like anything that will disturb their routine and composure.

Sounds are a particular concern for HSPs. They can perceive sounds and noises more prominently than most people. Music that is usual for us, may already be too loud for them. Certain beats which may be engaging and may even prod us to dance may be too violent or strong for their tolerance. Because of these excesses, HSPs are most likely to retreat from loud and sudden noises, preferring silence or calm music. There is a greater tendency for them to avoid high-traffic areas, parties, rock concerts or packed crowds. They may want to go to a supermarket when there are fewer people. They may live in quiet neighborhoods or a vacation in secluded off-beat tourist sites.

The sense of sight is a concern for HSPs. They are more particular in terms of the things they see. It may be an overreaction to the particular hue of an object, the brightness or darkness of a particular shade or simply the arrangement of patterns and colors on a landscape. They are actually good at artistic endeavors because of this sensitivity to details. But it can also be very tedious for them to have multi-sensory stimulation. Flashing or strobe lights may tire them easily. Flashy or neon colors may be too strong. They may even just prefer to rest in somber-colored interiors or plain walls so that their eyes can rest.

Inward stimuli are also very prominently felt by HSPs. They have a lower tolerance for pain than most people. A pinch may be slightly irritating for some but excruciating for HSPs. An upset stomach may warrant an immediate consult at the emergency room. HSPs easily consult for medical help when they feel sick or are in pain. They are very much in touch with how their body feels and will voice out concerns at the slightest pain. They are quick to recognize if their stomach is killing them, if their head is throbbing or a lump is bothering them. They are good patients because they will seek help at the onset of the disease.

These external and internal stimuli are magnified in the HSP. They will encounter a lot of problems because other people may not be as sensitive to these stimuli and may think that their concerns are too trivial to be taken seriously. Not many people will understand their concerns out of ignorance of what their condition is.

Next, HSPs are also very emotionally connected. They are in touch with their emotions and will display them more prominently than most people. Even with little stimuli, they can easily be ecstatic, saddened, angered or frightened. Their power to empathize with other people and situations is magnified as if the pain of others is also theirs. They may be too affected because of the stories they hear or movies they see. Events in their lives may also be heightened to the point of trauma. An unfortunate incident such as an accident, sickness or death may cause them to be deeply scarred or depressed. They may feel personal responsibility or guilt when negative events unfold.

Their reactions to these emotional upheavals may also be exaggerated, both in manifestation and duration. If the rest are just sad, they can be sobbing or inconsolable. They are the loudest to shriek at horror movies, or they may avoid watching it altogether. They may feel so much anger inside them, but they are more prone to restrain themselves, imploding silently. What other people may feel for moments or days will become weeks, months, or even years for HSPs. They may hold a grudge for a very long time, be affected by a sad story for weeks, or never recover from the death of a loved one. They feel as if these events have just happened recently, with the details ever fresh in their minds. But in one sense, they can also be advocates for causes. If they feel strongly about particular interests and concerns, they are going to make themselves heard. They will feel passionate about personal issues and rally people to support them.

Finally, HSPs have a tendency to adopt an inward approach. They prefer to reflect on their own or think of things longer and more thoroughly than others. They may be described as antisocial or shy because they would rather mull things on their own. They are more introverted, listening to their own feelings and tuning out the feelings of others. Instead of seeking help from outside, they are going to nurture their feelings and grapple with these on their own. They would prefer silence, not just because of the lack of auditory stimuli, but more because of the solitude required for thinking and reflecting.

Again, these observations on HSPs may not apply to everyone. Not all HSPs are shy but most would prefer to draw inwards. Not all HSPs may be sensitive to light, but most may have a certain sensitivity to a particular sensory stimulation. Each HSP is unique and different, expressing their sensitivity in their particular ways. You yourself may notice some hint of HSP in you, if not an outright HSP.

What causes people to become highly sensitive? A study by Acevedo, et al. (2018) has focused on a genetic-based trait called Sensory Processing Sensitivity which is more developed in HSPs. In this study, they were able to map out brain circuit patterns among people with HSP and compared it with the brain circuitry of those affected with Autism Spectrum Disorder, Schizophrenia, and Post-traumatic disorder. Results show that all these four conditions stimulate the precentral gyrus, a part of our brain that is involved in the conscious movement. Also, the caudate, thalamo-cingulate and default mode network which includes the temporal, parietal and angular gyrus were similarly activated in HSPs. These centers are responsible for reflective thinking, motor and cognitive control. This anatomical correlation may explain the fact that HSPs are more inward-looking and self-reflective, sensitive to their actions and the feelings of others.

But what distinguishes the sensory processing sensitivity in HSPs from the other pathological mental disorders is the activation of brain structures responsible for hormonal balance, calm, empathy, self-control and self-reflective thinking. This is an important distinguishing factor because HSPs are commonly mistaken to have schizophrenia or autism. Rather than having a scanty, loose memory as in schizophrenia, HSPs in fact have a good grasp of memory. They are also able to integrate their emotional, cognitive and sensory system unlike people with autism who tend to lack emotional intelligence. We emphasize here the fact that the anatomy of the brain of HSPs dictates the kind of behavior they display.

Understanding what being a highly sensitive person means is crucial in our approach to people, especially to children with this personality trait. They are not meant to be cured in the sense of taking away parts of their personality that may seem inconvenient for us. We have to understand that they are normal people who have a particular personality that is not shared by the greater majority of people. Their very anatomy dictates their difference in thinking, feeling, and behaving, so that they are inclined to be more sensitive than others. Future research is needed to understand the highly sensitive person in fuller detail. I hope I have given you an understanding of the topic of "highly sensitive person" and before we move on to the next chapter, I want to let you know that in this book, I will focus more on Highly Sensitive Children (HSC) and what you can do now so that they can thrive as adults in future.

Chapter 2

Celebrating the Gift

With such a personality trait, what should our approach be to HSCs? If we have a child that is highly sensitive, should we see his or her personality as a gift to celebrate or a curse we need to break? It is very difficult to raise children who are highly sensitive, especially if we do not have that personality ourselves. It is hard to understand their behavior because it does not fit in with the rest of society, that they will always be viewed as pushovers in schools and reclusive monks despising social relations. Having a highly sensitive child may even lead us to question ourselves, if we did something wrong during the pregnancy, if we raised them up too spoiled or too left to themselves, if we were bad parents.

The key here then is a radical perspective on HSCs, to view them not as a curse, but as a gift we should celebrate, discipline, handle and nurture. A "gift" is a good metaphor to describe HSCs because they should be sources of joy rather than disappointment, anxiety, or even fear. Gifts are blessings meant to make us happy, the kind of happiness that is not fleeting or fake. As parents, we never know what kind of children we will receive and so it is with HSC as gifts. They are not accidents in a pregnancy outcome or a product of poor child discipline at home. They are gifts that parents receive and should be celebrated, as with any child that is born. They may have some peculiarities, but it is those peculiarities that make them special.

It may not seem easy for parents to view their highly sensitive children as kids, especially if they become difficult to handle. But they are children nonetheless who just have different triggers and needs. In the course of trying to manage a high-maintenance child, you might overlook the fact that they have certain talents, abilities, and dispositions which are unique to them and will bring you a different kind of joy. The HSC changes the family dynamics, even binding the family together because of their unique capacity to tap into the emotion of people. They are heart people, wearing their emotions on their sleeves. And this is a good jumping point to highlight the special gifts and talents of highly sensitive children. I will now highlight some of the more prominent gifts highly sensitive children possess.

They Are Patient and Keen Listeners

It is actually not hard to discipline HSCs. You may be surprised by this because you may think that they are just simply high-maintenance children. On the contrary, HSCs are good listeners and followers. They have great respect for their parents and authority figures and will follow commands to the rule. This comes perhaps from their need to please people and satisfy that need to be seen as doing what is right. They may also be afraid of being punished. Older children who are highly sensitive turned out to be very responsible in taking care of their siblings. Even without your supervision, they will follow what you say. In that sense, they are actually low maintenance because they are easy to discipline.

Their listening ability is also uncanny for children their age. Since they are very particular to sound and emotions, HSCs would pick up all the details of whatever you say to them. If you tell them that you will pick them up at 5 PM, be sure to pick them up at the exact time because they will listen and follow exactly what you said. They are listening not just to what you say, but how you say things, and the underlying emotions embedded in each statement. If you tell them, "Honey not now," they will know if you are tired, angry, annoyed, or simply not in the mood by how you say the phrase. They listen to the small nuances of things said and unsaid and this is a good trait. They are able to sense how people are just by listening to them.

They Excel in School

In general, HSCs do well in school. The academic setting is a place where HSCs thrive because their skills are honed in this setting. School pushes students to be attentive and particular to details, expressive in language and methodical in logic. These are areas where the HSC does well. School also wants to develop independent learning; hence students are given a lot of homework or personal activities to test their skills and abilities. HSCs love this because they can be on their own, concentrating on the work and putting much thought on each item. Subjects such as arts, language, reading and comprehension are fields where they excel because they have good attention to detail. They know how to mix colors and copy images on paper. They are particular to expressions in language and their memory is extensive. But they will also do well in Science and Math. The thought process involved in logic is something HSCs can be known for.

HSCs would encounter challenges to education when it comes to collaborative work and time management. They would prefer to work alone, but the school will often have activities that are team-based. School also trains children to work with each other, whether in projects or academic papers. And HSCs would have a hard time jelling in with other children because they have a particular way of doing things. They would either hog up all the work or have minimal participation. Their attention to detail is also something that can be tiresome for them. They can be perfectionists, unable to move on until the details are all perfect. And this can be time-consuming. The work is excellent, but it will take a lot of time. HSCs then won't thrive in time-pressured activities and exams because they like to take their time. But in general, HSCs would regard teachers as their ally and will excel in the school setting.

They Have a Sense of How People Around Them Are Feeling

HSCs will also be very sensitive to you and your family members' feelings. They can pick your emotional thermometer through your words and actions, and even the things you don't say and do. If you had a bad day in the office, they can sense right away and will steer clear from you. If you are generally happy and carefree, they can also sense this and will warm up to you easily. If you need a hug, they can sense that and will hug away all your pains and problems away. HSCs are very endearing children with high emotional intelligence. They can anticipate appropriate behavior based on the feelings projected to them.

HSCs then also make good friends. They can easily navigate the complexities of friendships and feelings. They know when their friends are fighting with each other, when they are developing crushes, or when they are having heartbreaks. They are the go-to-person when it comes to complex personal problems because they are able to analyze situations and empathize with people very easily. They can dish out advice that is grounded on sound judgment. They are patient listeners, able to sift between the emotions people feel when they tell their stories. With their keen observance of people, they can spot personality flaws and probable causes of problems. People depend on HSCs for advice, making them the best friend you always wanted to have.

They Are Quiet

This is actually a rare gem to find among children and a practical gift you can be thankful for. Unlike other children, HSCs are inward-directed and will require a lot of silence. The silence is a space for them to gather their own emotions, listen to their body, allows them to imagine and create their own world. They are good listeners and observers of people because they are silent enough to let their senses work optimally. This does not mean that they are antisocial. They will relate to others and even be talkative at times when asked. They just have a preference for being quiet, and active when needed.

As children, parents appreciate this silence because it creates a calm atmosphere in the house. People are able to relax because HSCs demand calmness in silence. They may be prone to tantrums and meltdowns, but these are rare occasions and often triggered by a particular concern. But for most of the time, they can be depended on to learn quietly, listen attentively and think independently. If you are not comfortable with silence, then this could be a problem for you. But silence itself is a gift you should explore and even inculcate in your own life as parents. You will do well to learn from your highly sensitive child how to be quiet yourself in order to be more self-reflective and attuned to your feelings.

They Are Very Thoughtful in Creative Ways

Being good listeners and emotionally connected, HSCs are also very thoughtful. They spend a lot of time composing what they want to say and usually, these are emotional statements that are well-thought-out. They can give honest compliments to people they appreciate. They are able to say negative things in a constructive way because they put effort into not hurting people with words. They will anticipate your needs and please you even before you ask for them. They are the ones who usually write cards on your birthday or on occasions such as Christmas, your anniversary, or Mothers' or Fathers' day. When it comes to their siblings, they want to make sure everyone feels good and appreciated. They will go to lengths to buy gifts for their siblings or to encourage them to do well in school.

HSCs are also very creative children. Give them paint and they will draw, a guitar and they will play, singing lessons and they will perform. These creative activities rely so much on attention to detail which they are good at. They love colors and are experimental on how they can make good drawings and patterns. Their inner world is also powerful due to their imagination. This helps them create characters, paintings, music that is novel and interesting. The punch comes when they use art to channel their feelings. If they feel angry, they may displace this in a canvass. If they are ecstatic, they can burst into song. They are not afraid to show their feelings and talents. When you notice their interest, develop that further because they are going to thrive in that area.

Chapter 3

Handling the Gift

ell

It is true that we must appreciate our highly sensitive children as gifts and celebrate their talents and abilities. But these gifts also come with a few challenges. Like any other child, HSCs will also have their mood swings and personality quirks. Again, I emphasize that all children will have certain difficulties, whether it is in behavior, attitude, mental development, or communication skills. There is no perfect child all the time. Taking care of HSCs will be no different than handling a regular child who may be sweet at one time and then bawling in another. What we want to highlight here are some of the challenges parents may encounter when taking care of an HSC. Being sensitive people, HSCs will present with particular difficulties that parents should be prepared to handle. HSCs can be exhausting to manage especially if you don't understand what is making them behave the way they do. You may get frustrated with them, but by anticipating their meltdowns, you can conserve your energy and expectations better as well as become more patient with them.

HSCs Are Prone to Tantrums and Meltdowns

Sigmund Freud, the father of psychology, introduced the concept of the id, the ego, and the super-ego. He theorizes that all of us have these three components, influencing our behaviors. The id is the part of our consciousness that deals with our desires and wants. The id controls our need to seek pleasure. The super-ego is the part of our consciousness responsible for obeying rules and commandments. It is in direct contrast to the id which has no regard for conventions. The ego integrates the id and the super-ego together, deciding whether we should follow our wants or follow what is right according to social standards. The three components all work to influence what kind of choices we make on a daily basis.

HSCs are a furball of feelings and emotions. They are so in touch with them that they may have problems expressing what they feel inside. As children, they will be pure id, the part of our brain that follows the wants without regard for anything. If they feel anything, they will express it without being conscious if their behavior is appropriate or not. They may even create a scene in public when they get into a tantrum. It may be difficult to calm down, no matter how much you sweet-talk or even scold them. When the id is released, it will be very hard to control.

What are the usual things that set off HSCs? Each HSC will have a trigger unique to them and to the circumstance. They are easily affected more than other kids because they are so in touch with themselves and with their feelings. Any simple thing such as not getting the toy they want, not being allowed a certain activity, fighting with their siblings, a lost item they love, too much noise or any other extreme sensory experience may trigger a tantrum. Just like ordinary kids, HSCs will want to have their own way and have a hard time processing the different emotions they feel when they get rejected.

But what is particular to HSCs compared to other kids is the degree and length of time they can keep on having a tantrum or a meltdown. In terms of degree, their reactions can be rather exaggerated. Their fits can be disproportionate to the behavior they are reacting to. A simple "No" to their request can send them crashing on the floor. They will also take their time processing and feeling their emotions. If they are sulking from you, they will do so for a good length of time. They may not show their feelings on the external surface, but they may be nourishing a grudge for a long time. These meltdowns can even interfere with their daily activities such as school.

HSCs May Be Particular and Picky About Personal Items

HSCs have a certain way of proceeding and routine that they are particular to. They may fix their things in a certain way. They may have a particular way of eating their food or a particular texture of fabric they are comfortable with. They may be meticulous about the way they look or conscious of the brand of items they purchase. These routines are set and give the HSCs a certain sense of safety and predictability. If you disturb that rhythm, then you will really cross an HSC. If you mess up their cabinet or accidentally read through their private writings, then you will feel a lot of aggression from them. They have a strong sense of privacy and possession, taking good care of their things. If you cross their boundaries, then they will retaliate as though they feel attacked. They may even have a hard time trusting you a second time if you offend their sensibilities in any way.

Schooling may often be challenging for highly sensitive children. Though they excel in academics and individual work, the school setting itself may present certain difficulties for them. HSCs may have a particular way of learning or doing things that the teacher may not be able to provide. Socialization with other children will also be very tricky for them. Loud voices or strong personalities may antagonize HSCs, which influences class dynamics. Though the teacher cannot control all these factors, they should be guided as to how HSCs can learn better.

HSCs Have Difficulty Handling Negative Feedback

As with other children, HSCs will also commit mistakes. They may miss out on homework, may become unruly in class, or may exceed set video game times. As parents, your role is to discipline your children, giving feedback in a manner that is understandable for them so that they can stop doing behaviors you feel are not appropriate. The issue of feedback is very sensitive for HSCs. It is not because they are perfectionists who have high self-esteem and will take it hard if they commit mistakes. Rather, HSCs are so in touch with their emotions that negative feedback would be taken hard. You will scare them off if you suddenly burst into a raging sermon or even a wallop on their behind. They fear offending you more than anything. HSCs also tend to make things personal. When their work is deemed a "B+", they may also think that they are "B+" people, not good enough for the standards of teachers or of parents. They have difficulty separating their personhood from their work and output, so that an attack on their work is an attack on their person. You have to be careful then on giving them feedback. Deliberate well your choice of words because they need that feedback even if it is painful. But you can package it in a way that is less offending to them or will only focus on the output or behavior and not their person.

Giving feedback is as difficult for them as receiving feedback. Because they are easily hurt by negative comments, HSCs will also think of the other's feelings when they are giving feedback. They can spend hours crafting a feedback that is direct but not offending. They will expend a lot of effort, revising comments and approaches just to consider the other's feelings. In this way, they are very thoughtful. But the length of time they take to give out the comment may sometimes be too prolonged. It is actually good to get feedback from an HSC because you are sure that it is well thought out. But it will create unnecessary stress on the HSC just to give you the perfect feedback.

HSCs Are Targets of Bullying

With a heightened sensibility, a well-spring of emotions, and particularity with details, HSCs are easy targets for bullying. We see this very much in the school-age, where socialization happens with other kids. You cannot blame other children for not understanding HSCs because they are also exploring how they express themselves to others. But these interactions may often lead to abuses since HSCs may not fit in to certain cliques of children. They can be bullied for their peculiarities such as the way they dress, their fussiness on details, or seemingly weak characters. Some HSCs actually retaliate but that still opens the door for more bullying. Children are still finding their talents and abilities and exploring their social skills. HSCs also desire to belong to particular groups, but the school setting messes up with their preferred order of socialization. You have to be very vigilant in terms of observing for signs of bullying in your HSC. They can be verbally abused through name-calling or cursing. There could be instances of physical abuse when young people get out of hand. Rather than confide in you, they may just clam up and brood over their feelings.

It might also benefit us to discuss this bully-bullied relationship and how it can develop in school. I have to say that nobody is born a bully or a bullied. It is not a genetic trait that we pass on to our children. Most bullies are aggressive, but there are also cases of passive-aggressiveness that are as insidious as the direct ones. Bullying is brought about by the process of socialization, where personalities clash and aggressions are tested. Children are all different from each other, having different tastes and likes, looks, and origins. As such, diversity opens the door for the desire of some groups to establish a certain norm. This desire is very strong in teenagers where they want to belong to certain groups so they can fit in. If individuals don't fit into the standards set by the group, they can be antagonized through bullying. Bullies hate diversity and will desire only that their standards are the only ones to be followed. Bullies think that they have a monopoly on how to dress and behave, how to play games, and who gets to win. It is an issue of power, held by people who are just beginning to know who they are. The HSC, who epitomizes diversity, is the natural target of bullies because they don't fit in. HSCs are not part of the majority because they may be too shy or withdrawn into their own world. They have the capacity to retaliate, but the bullying may persist. The relationship between the bullies and the bullied persist because the bully draws power from overcoming the bullied. Once the bullied HSC realizes that he or she can afford not to give that power, then the relationship may be broken. When they stand up for themselves, HSCs are able to destroy the cycle of bullying.

HSCs May Be Secretive

The inner world of the HSC is the place where they feel safest. It is an environment where they can be themselves without being judged or pressured by others. It is both a thinking and an emotional space, a place where they brood over things they learned or process feelings which occur to them. You will find them mostly silent or staring dreamily into space as they are absorbed in their inner world. On the one hand, this is a good personality trait since it develops their sense of self-awareness and identity. By being self-reflective, they are able to get to know themselves better and plan out how best to interact with others. But on the other hand, the inner world may be an escape from encountering other people. When HSCs feel threatened, they are going to withdraw to their inner space, afraid to confront the stressor and resolve the issue. This is a coping mechanism they have developed because they have learned that by being silent, they can shut out the problems.

This will become pathological when the HSC encounters problems that they cannot solve on their own. Because they are naturally drawn to their inner world, HSCs can be secretive, nourishing their own thoughts and feelings to themselves. They will refuse to share with others their thoughts, feelings, and problems because they feel they are judged. If they have a problem in school, they will try to solve it on their own. If they have relationship problems, they will keep to themselves. If they are having issues with their gender and sexuality, peer pressure problems, issues with other family members, they will not open up easily. This is difficult because the problem at hand does not get discussed and is not solved immediately. Because HSCs are non-confrontational, sometimes, the problems become worse. You have to be very vigilant because the exclusive preoccupation of HSCs with themselves can already be signs that they are depressed or anxious, or even suicidal. They will only let you in if they trust you or if it is already too late. Watch out for danger signs when you feel that your highly sensitive child suddenly becomes secretive beyond the usual.

Chapter 4

Disciplining the Gift

It is good that we accept our highly sensitive children for what they are, affirming their skills and talents and providing them with opportunities for growth and self-awareness. This goes the same for any child that you may have. But, your duty as parents is still to form your children to become responsible adults on their own, capable of making well-discerned decisions and being able to function in all aspects of life. You still have to instill some form of discipline in your children, especially because they are still developing and capable of being molded. Being an HSC does not mean you have to give special treatments all the time. Yes, they have particularities that they are possessive of. But this does not mean you can simply tolerate excess or condone bad behavior. In fact, disciplining them may be the best way you can help them survive now and later on as adults.

I have formed some general guidelines on how to discipline your highly sensitive child. From the previous chapter, we note that HSCs have a tendency to deal poorly with negative feedback. But this is not an excuse not to give them what you think is right for them. Be courageous, because as a parent, you would want to equip your child with all the skills and resilience they will need when they become independent. Combine a lot of patience with gentle firmness so that you don't antagonize your highly sensitive child but still discipline him or her well.

Establish Rules

As with all your children, it is important for you to establish rules in the house. When you lay down the rules, you are teaching your children the value of keeping boundaries. These boundaries are not meant to make your kids uncomfortable or to repress their freedom. Rather, these boundaries are meant for them to enjoy themselves in the best and most productive way possible. Parents have a hard time establishing and enforcing rules because they also grew up in households that either have no rules or have too strict rules. Our own experience of house rules will actually determine the kind of rules we will enforce in our house. But since some of us have bad experiences of disciplining, it is best to understand what kind of rules will work best.

One quality of a rule is that it must be clear. When parents tell their children any rule, the rule must be very clear and delineated. If you tell your children that they should be home by night, they will be very confused. Does it mean that they have to be in the house when it gets dark? Can they stretch it to midnight? Is 4 AM still considered night? But if you formulate your rule as they should be home by 6 PM, then the rule becomes very clear. Rules that are vague will be subject to a lot of interpretations and you will end up becoming defensive and authoritarian.

The second characteristic of a good rule is that it should be reasonable. Your rule must make some sense, even to a child. The worst thing a parent can say to their children when asked why the children should do a chore is that "just because I say so." This is said when parents are exhausted to teach their children the logic behind the task or the chore they are being made to do. As parents, we should do our best to explain to our children why we do the things we do in the capacity that they can understand. When you tell them to make up their bed, you have to explain the value of cleanliness and having an ordered room and not just brush the question off with "Just do it." When they ask you why they have to stop watching television or play video games after an hour, do your best to explain to them the value of time management and even disconnecting from devices in order to interact with real people. They will not understand everything all at once. But when you are not defensive and children see that they can ask you questions without being brushed off, the following of rules becomes easier.

The final characteristic of a good rule is that it should be communicated clearly. You don't invent rules on the spot when it is convenient for you. You don't impose rules that only you can understand. These are quite self-explanatory, but you would be surprised at how poor some parents can be in explaining rules to their children. In their mind, they already know that they have told their children not to touch or use their personal items. But in truth, they have only mumbled it off in passing or explained it in vague terms. When their children tamper with their personal items, they fly into a rage and the children can get traumatized. You have to make sure that you state your rules in a manner that is understandable to your children. Ask them to repeat your rule after you said it. Test if they really remember your rules. You can only discipline them when they have understood your rule and still violated it. But until then, you cannot make them responsible for breaking rules you have not communicated properly.

The next part of establishing rules is enforcing them. You don't just make rules and not follow them up with execution. Rules are there so that the children will keep them. When you enforce rules, you have to be firm. They only become rules when children sense your authority in enforcing them. If you say the curfew is at 6 PM, then it is 6 PM, not 6:30 PM, not 7 PM. If you strongly feel that these are rules your children will need later on in life, then start them early with discipline.

Part of discipline, is, of course, making your children realize that their actions have consequences. Each parent will have their own style of disciplining their children in this regard. Some come from backgrounds where physical abuse such as spanking and belting are the norm. I do not judge the way you discipline your children. I will only recommend those that I personally feel worked with my own children and have seen it work on other children with better results. When you discipline your child, make sure that the punishment is proportionate to the task. When they commit a mistake, the consequence must be proportionate to the error. The power of punishment is when children can see that the punishment is graded according to the severity. If they fail in a subject, perhaps they are not allowed certain privileges until the next grading. If they get into a fight that resulted in being in detention, then they may not go out with friends for a month. These simple measures send a message that you are serious and that the destructive behavior of your children must be stopped. Also, allow for a system of warnings before you give a punishment. Give them a first warning for a first offense, a second warning for the next, and deal the punishment on the third. In this way, you are teaching children the value of second chances. Children will know their boundaries because they have been warned. But the most important advice on discipline is that you should communicate with your children. Explain to them the relationship between the bad behavior they did and the corresponding consequence. They need to understand or else they will keep on doing the same mistake while holding a grudge with you.

HSCs will need a good set of rules in order to behave properly. Like any other child, they will commit mistakes and break some rules. Try explaining consequences to them so that they can take negative feedback properly. Do not be soft on them because they will also need to be resilient at some point. Just make sure that your discipline is proportionate to the amount of learning they can get from the punishment. Remember that the goal of discipline is not to punish but to teach children how to behave properly.

Encourage Open Communication

HSCs are naturally withdrawn and secretive. But the behavior will only persist when they feel that they cannot trust others with their secrets or that they will be judged. If you establish a space where they can be safe and comfortable to be with themselves, then you will be able to enter their inner world. If you make this a general rule in the house where everyone has to abide, then your highly sensitive child will also learn to trust his or her siblings. Being open and honest with each other is a family culture that parents are responsible for establishing. When given the chance, HSCs actually like to share, especially if it is about feelings. They would want to share their feelings as well as get to know the feelings of others. In this way, your child will not have to be secretive and confide in others you may not trust. The whole family also benefits from open communication because there is greater bonding brought about by mutual trust and respect.

Allow open communication, especially when they commit mistakes. When children commit an error or break a rule, there is a tendency to hide it from parents because they will be punished. They may have experiences where you burst out in anger or you even physically hit them because they committed an infraction. Do not traumatize your children. There should be a healthy approach to committing mistakes so that you still get to correct the behavior but at the same, encourage open communication. Focus on the act that you want to correct and not on the person who committed it. Explain to your child that you are withdrawing privileges, not because he or she is a bad person, but because what he did was not good. By depersonalizing the behavior, you can still extend your love to your child and, at the same time, discipline him or her. The next time, children will feel that they can report to you their mistakes and own up to them. This already signifies that they are becoming responsible for their actions and are open to receiving the consequences. The corrective process then becomes formative for your children.

Involve Them in Housework

I found that doing housework is one of the foundations of a responsible adult. When you make your children do housework, you are building a character that will make them into responsible adults in the future. In a practical sense, this is convenient because you don't need to do a lot of things on your own. But at the same time, there is character formation going on when you involve them in housework. When children wash plates, make their beds, clean up after playing, throw trash in the proper wastebasket, you are instilling in them essential lessons they will bring to their own families and workplace. The house is the best place to learn hard work, good hygiene and etiquette, and good manners and self-discipline. Children will normally complain and you might be softened by their tantrums. But you are an adult and you have the power to mold them into constructive activities that will benefit your children in the future.

Housework is especially formative for HSCs. Involve them in household chores that they are capable of. They may initially refuse and go into tantrums. But once they see your insistence on the household chores, they will follow. From the following, they can learn how these small acts can benefit them as they grow in independence from their parents. Let them sweat it out as they clean their room so they can appreciate the value of hard work. Let them wash dishes so they can learn the value of hygiene. Let them pick up their toys and put them in the proper area so they can be responsible for taking care of their own things. When you do these chores together, you are even telling them that they are part of the family. HSCs can be self-absorbed and when they are drawn out by doing chores, they can realize how equally important it is to do things with other people.

Challenge Perceptions

Just because they are reflective and self-withdrawn does not mean that HSCs are always right. They may think a lot about something they learned in school or they may be bothered by a movie they saw and form an opinion about it. But it does not automatically mean that their opinions are balanced or even correct. They are children and they are still in the process of forming their own opinions, observing adults, and making sense of their world. HSCs have the advantage of being more introspective than their peers. But they may often times base their judgment and opinions on their own perspective. As such, the information they hold may be incomplete or even faulty.

To help them with this, encourage your highly sensitive child to expand his or her perspective. Do not tell them outright that they are wrong. Tell them that they can consider a different opinion or even an opposite one. If they strongly despise a classmate, challenge that opinion by telling your kid to look at the perspective of the other child. If they have strong opinions against a certain movie or dislike a particular teacher, challenge them by guiding them to think about the other person's feelings. In this way, their opinions are still their own but have expanded in terms of variety. By encouraging them to take the perspective of the other, you are actually drawing them out of their shell and into a healthy relationship with other people.

Coordinate With School

Make your child's school your ally. HSCs are prone to be bullied and you cannot be there the whole time to watch over them or to ward off their bullies. In this regard, the school becomes the second parent and has the responsibility for your children while they are in the vicinity. In order to help your child, get feedback from your child's teacher. The teacher is the best person who knows your child because he or she sees your child most of the day. They know class dynamics and how your child copes with the different stresses. They are then in the best position to give objective feedback on your child. They will also report to you if your child is being bullied and how he or she is handling the situation. The goal here is not to put a camera in the classroom but to seek out an ally in forming children.

Educate your teachers about what a highly sensitive child is. This is not to demand special treatment or even to make teachers pity your child. You should also be an advocate in letting other people, especially teachers, know about this particular personality type. When they understand HSCs more, teachers can actually cater their lessons so that HSCs can learn optimally. You can explain to your teacher that the child learns better by using pictures or that they are particular about loud noises. But you have to trust that teachers will do their best to educate your child as well as other children. The teacher is not just caring for one special student but is taking care of the whole. By educating teachers, you are giving them as much information as you can to help them see the whole class and to create a safe environment where children can learn.

Chapter 5

Nurturing the Gift

~ele~

Highly sensitive children have been described to be orchids compared to other children who are dandelions. This means that HSCs thrive only in certain controlled environments and will wither when placed in harsh spaces. If you push them too much in going to sports and playing basketball with their peers when it is not their interest, you will only isolate them and crush their spirit. If you only let them do the things that they want to do, then they may become spoiled and dependent on you, unable to function in other aspects of society without your presence. A good mix of loving discipline, firm guidance, and relaxed patience will certainly make your child bloom. Here are some points to consider when you are beginning to appreciate and nourish the gift of an HSC.

Accept Them

The best way you can ever take care of an HSC is to accept your child unconditionally. Tell them that they are beautiful, inside and out. Hug them constantly and make them feel special. When HSCs feel that they are accepted, they will become their best selves for you. When you love them unconditionally, they will want to love you back and others too, with the same openness and respect as you showered them. This may be rather obvious but often, acceptance is not the first instinct of a parent with a highly sensitive child. They can be confused with the gift, exhausted by their tantrums, and even critical of their thoughts and opinions. When you begin treating your child as a problem to be solved, they will remain unsolvable and elusive. Your child will be more guarded with you and will not open up their feelings to you because they feel threatened. Give them the acceptance that you also give to your other children.

In accepting the gift, do not compare it with the other gifts. If you have other children, nothing is more hurtful than comparing them to each other. If your older child excels in sports and the HSC does not, do not tell them to be more like their older sibling. This comparison game is unfair to everyone and sets standards on your children that they do not need and harms their own growth. Your HSC will bring this into their adult lives, debasing themselves because they are not enough for you and will not be enough for any other standard. They will inherit this comparative behavior and repeat this deforming attitude to their own children. Stop comparing your children. Tell your HSC that they should just be more of themselves. Your children are all different from each other, though they may look the same. What binds them together is your unconditional love for all of them. In this way, the HSC will learn to appreciate their uniqueness and will not be ashamed of being different.

Establish a Routine

Create a schedule you can follow on a daily basis. For example, you can set a wake-up time for 7 AM. Your children should be making their beds, brushing their teeth then shower up afterward. Breakfast at 8 and off to school. Pick up kids at 4 PM, free time until dinner at 7 PM. Wash plates, have a shower, and off to bed. Routines. You might not appreciate the power of routines especially if you have an erratic schedule. But routines are valuable to HSCs because they give them a sense of control. The predictability of the breakfast in the morning, the assurance of school, the fixedness of bedtime all give a sense of calmness in a highly sensitive child. Because they know which activities will happen at particular times, they feel relaxed and are able to be themselves. There is even anticipation of events which makes them excited if they like that activity. They can prepare for exams or tests that are routine, so their stress level is controlled. Routines make for a good disposition and good preparation.

When you disturb the routine, they can get flustered and lost. Surprises in the routines can be very stressful. The stress abates when they find a familiar face or event. If you miss picking them up from school at 4 PM, they will start panicking. If they stay up too late at night, they may be sleepy the following day. If you need to leave suddenly for a business trip which they don't know, they can feel very uncomfortable. Small glitches in the routine may foster some sense of resilience as HSCs are forced to deal with the situation. But prolonged unpredictability can cause them severe stress they may not be able to cope adequately. Routines then are very therapeutic for HSCs.

Encourage Their Interests and Talents

HSCs are one of the most creative and talented of personality traits. Because of their attention to detail, to the way colors are mixed, to the composition of images and the progression of notes, HSCs are natural artists. Encourage them to explore their talents by enrolling them in workshops, buying them art tools and crafts, bringing them to museums. Children are at an age where they need constant stimulation. The mind is still very plastic and will develop only to the extent that it is used. So, good exposure to the arts may open creative channels for your child. They may not exhibit good artistry at first, but by mere exposure, they may grow into the creative process. Encourage your child if he wants to play an instrument, write a short story, take good pictures or dabble in clothes-making. It is exciting to care for an HSC because a genius may just be in front of you.

Not all HSCs, of course, will thrive in the arts. Interests of HSCs can be as varied as sports, math and sciences, wall climbing, engineering, skateboarding, or computer programming. Each child will be as different from the other but support them all just the same. You or your child may initiate the exploration of an interest. The more that you expose your child, the more information he or she has of what he or she is good at or wants. If your child has a strong objection to a particular activity, don't push them too hard. You may want your child to thrive in a particular field, but if that is not what he wants, then he will do poorly in it. As parents, we can only help our kids in exploring their own passions. But we cannot make them passionate about something by forcing them on it. Let them discover who they really are on their own guided by our loving support.

Respect Their Personal Space

If you have taught them the value of boundaries in house rules, also be respectful of the HSCs own personal space. As introspective people as they are, HSCs will be very territorial when it comes to their space, whether physical or emotional. The personal space gives them a sense of calmness and peace because it is a place where they will not be judged for being themselves. This is a space where they can mull over their feelings into its fullest extent. You may be very concerned about what they are thinking and feeling. But you have to give your children the space where they can be themselves without your prying. Yes, there is open communication in the family. But there should also be spaces for private thoughts and feelings. You may be invited to this inner space, but you cannot force your child to divulge all of his secrets.

Respecting personal space involves protecting a safe distance from the common space to your child's place. Do not read your children's diaries because that is theirs. Do not eavesdrop on their conversation or stalk them at school to see if they have friends you trust. Stop being helicopter parents always snooping at your kids. They will tell you when they feel that they can trust you, not when they are threatened to be honest. Trust is not something you demand from your children, but rather, something you earn, even if they are just children.

Involve the Whole Family

Unless you are a solo parent, the joy and burden of raising a highly sensitive child do not depend on you alone. There is great joy in sharing the challenges and genius of HSC with others. As a couple, it is not only the mother who has the task to take care of the child. Both mother and father are equally responsible for disciplining their children as well as enjoying their company. You or your spouse may be working. But you should also learn how to balance your work with taking care of a highly sensitive child because the attention demand may be higher in them compared to most kids. When highly sensitive children are throwing tantrums and you feel too exhausted to the point of screaming at the child, stop yourself and let the other partner take over. When you are too busy to attend school activities, involve your other half so that the child still feels attended to. This delicate flower only grows when both parents are there to make him feel loved.

The dynamics of siblings are also a factor in raising a highly sensitive child. If your child is an only child, then they may have a tendency to be absorbed in their inner world and deal only with others during school. But when they have other siblings, HSCs will have to interact with them, adjusting themselves to each other's temperaments and personalities, getting into fights, and enjoying games together. Involve your other children when you are taking care of an HSC. It is not so much giving special attention to the point of neglecting the other children. You just want to make the other children aware of their sibling's particular needs and to be more conscious of them. The HSC is a gift to everyone because they can tap into the emotions of the family and bind them together. When a family works in harmony to take care of a highly sensitive child, they are brought closer to each other and become more sensitive themselves.

Chapter 6

Growing With the Gift

At this point, you may have some idea of how to take care of your highly sensitive child. They are challenging to take care of, but the rewards far outweigh the stress. When you see your child thriving in school or confiding secrets with you, there is a sense that you have done something right in raising your kids. Celebrate those moments because these are times when you become affirmed of your calling to become parents. Seeing them grow is like harvesting the fruits and enjoying a well-earned bounty.

But your highly sensitive child will not always be a child. They will grow into their own persons, choosing their own careers, picking their own partners, starting their own families, and living their own lives. As parents, you can only be there to support them when this happens. Our duties as parents never end but only change from an active to a supportive kind of parenting. We are partly responsible for their adulthood because the way we take care of them as children determines the kind of people they will become. But HSCs, in general, will have specific challenges in adulthood they will encounter. By knowing these challenges, you can anticipate what kind of preparations you can do so they will be equipped to conquer these challenges.

Becoming Independent Adults

The issue of self-dependence is very real to adults with HSCs. Two extremes in parenting may develop two extreme forms of attachment in adult HSCs. If the parenting type is very cold and distant, where the parents are hard on discipline and cannot tolerate the tantrums of a highly sensitive child, then the adult HSC may become as cold and distant. They will have difficulty opening up to other people because their own experiences of family and parents have not been enriching. They will grow up as mistrustful of other people with low self-esteem because they have been subjected to much criticism growing up. Some, of course, are able to resist this pattern, but only with much effort. The destructiveness of a cold parenting style will traumatize the HSC until adulthood.

On the other hand, if the parenting style is more of spoiling the child, giving them whatever they want all of the time, then no discipline is learned. Adult HSCs will become very dependent on their parents who have become their sources of consolation and safety. When they feel stressed, their parents will solve problems for them. When they want luxury, their parents will provide for them. When they need something, their parents will be at hand. When the parents are less able to provide, the adult HSC will be mortified that he or she has to face life on his own. The adjustment to adulthood is difficult because they are used to being provided and cared for. It will take some time before they can establish themselves outside of their parents' identities.

The sweet spot is knowing the balance between a disciplined parenting and a loving one, making it a disciplined loving parenting style. In this kind of setup, parents raise their children with a lot of unconditional love, providing for them in the measure that they can. But there is also a premium for discipline, where children are given boundaries and made to realize consequences for their actions. With a disciplined loving parenting style, parents will raise responsible adults who are independent and trusting of other people. They will know how to be intimate with other people, but they will recognize boundaries. They will replicate the kind of parenting you gave them to their own children. So, there is a big burden to really discipline and love your kids at the same time.

Establishing Intimate and Professional Relationships

We can never escape relating with others as we grow old. The family and school already set up this socialization process. When individuals transition to adulthood, the interaction evolves to include professional relationships and even intimate ones. After school, your children will have to take up jobs whether as employees, entrepreneurs, doctors, lawyers, or whoever they want to be. But those areas will still involve a lot of interaction with other people. As professionals, HSCs can bring a lot of connectedness in groups. They will do well in creative positions, art professions, or those that involve artistic expressions such as advertising. With their emotional insight, they will do well as counselors, psychiatrists, and medical professionals. They may not thrive too well in professions that are too technical and lack a lot of emotional connectedness. In terms of blending with other people, HSCs must be able to give a good sense of themselves, a solid grasp of their identity. They must be aware of what they want, what conditions will trigger their stress, what kind of work they can tolerate, which personalities they can gel with. With a good sense of self, the adult HSC may establish himself as different from others yet comfortable with it. If the HSC fails to become self-aware, then he will always try to adjust himself to what others want him to be. This can be a tiring process of trying to fit in which will cause a lot of stress.

In terms of workload, HSCs must guard themselves in terms of stress management. They have a tendency to overwork themselves and this can cause burnout. If you mix persona, family, and professional problems, then they can burst and simply shoot off. In order to prevent this burnout, HSCs must be self-aware as to their limits and how to cope with stress once they feel overburdened. They will naturally retreat to themselves and this is their way of recharging energy. They may not be the ones who like to party away to unload stress but would rather have a quiet dinner and a good sleep to get ready for the next day. Stress management is needed for HSCs to thrive in the workplace.

Intimate relationships are also a concern for HSCs. They can rather be good at it because they have a good sense of the emotional connection with another person. They may fall in love easily and wear their hearts on their sleeves. But they can also be fooled easily when people take advantage of them. These rollercoasters of feelings can be exhausting for them and they may think twice when entering new relationships. People who have dated HSCs say that they are thoughtful and sensitive on the one hand but may also be demanding for others. Once an HSC finds a suitable partner, their energy goes into dedicating themselves to their partners and to the family they will form. They will always be the more emotional ones, whether that is good or bad at the moment. Through a lot of experiences, they may learn how to channel that emotional intuitiveness to optimal use in intimate relationships.

Mental Illness and HSC

The strong inner world of the HSC makes them susceptible to a lot of mental illnesses. They get stressed easily and maybe fragile in terms of receiving negative feedback. All of these stressors could easily pile up in their unconscious, multiplying by the minute in their mind. When they have reached their limit in repressing all these negative emotions, they become very vulnerable to a number of mental illnesses manifesting in their teenage years down to their adult lives. Because they are very secretive in nature, they may be prone to depression as they would want to keep their issues to themselves. For fear of offending other people, HSCs would simply mope over their frustrations on their own. This cycle of thinking negatively about the world, of others and of themselves becomes a loop in their mind. Without intervention, they can easily succumb to depression.

Since they are also very emotional, significant negative milestones can deeply affect HSCs. Deaths in the family, sickness, unfortunate events and rejections may be so ingrained in them they will have a hard time moving on. Their current activities may be hampered because of a trauma in the past. This leads them to be susceptible to post-traumatic stress disorder. Small triggers about the traumatic event can already set them in an exaggerated behavior which is often self-destructive. As adults, HSCs need to toughen themselves and watch out that their emotions don't control them and their social functioning.

Anxiety will always be marked in HSC. This stems from their bullied past, where they had to go to school and confront all those bullies. They simply graduate from school but in their adulthood, bullies and the bullied still exist. HSCs still take on the role of the bullied and the anxiety that comes with it. They fear being judged, they anticipate negative events, and they always think about a grim future, the HSC may succumb to generalized anxiety disorder. Through reasoning out and proper relaxation techniques such as returning to their routine, HSCs can cope with these life stressors and lessen the anxiety they work themselves up on their own.

It does not mean that being an HSC will make you mentally ill. There are a lot of HSCs who are able to cope well with stressors and live integrated lives. What I am saying is that given the nature of HSCs, they have a higher chance of acquiring these mental illnesses compared to the general population. HSCs must begin by understanding what ails or stresses them and find ways to cope in a healthy, life-giving way.

Conclusion

It is not easy to have a highly sensitive child who may have a lot of demands. You might be blaming yourself for producing a child who cries easily, who is frequently bullied or who goes into inconsolable tantrums. You may even think that giving them birth is a mistake. Stop worrying. Your dilemma is very much unwarranted and comes from not knowing who your child is and how beautiful and blessed they are. Having an HSC as a child is a gift you should treasure. Not everyone would want such a gift given the many complexities it possesses. But when you are lucky enough to have one, be thankful. There are many talents and abilities locked inside your child. They have a great power to connect people through a deep insight into their emotions. HSCs are very thoughtful and mindful of how people are feeling. They make sure you feel good and that the family is bonded together. Always remind yourself that having a highly sensitive child is a gift you should nurture and develop.

Hopefully, you have learned a lot about how to take care of your highly sensitive child. Remember that at the end of the day, you have to be patient with them. There is a slow process of formation happening each day. With your steady guidance, your highly sensitive child will bloom on their own. You may not see the changes right away or on a daily basis. They often bloom when you least expect it. Wait lovingly on your highly sensitive child and you will be rewarded magnificently. How you care for your child now will determine the kind of highly sensitive adult they will be in the future. So, invest in caring for them now and reap much joy as you watch them grow.

About Author

Freeda is a bestselling author who has written multiple books on parenting and family life. She knows that raising children can be tough, but it's also one of the most rewarding experiences any parent can ever have. She has devoted her life to understanding the psychology behind good parenting and shares what she's learned with others through her books, blogs, and newsletters.

She is also a mother of a highly sensitive child. Freeda shares her story not just to help other parents learn how to raise a highly sensitive child but also to impart lessons on what helped her get through the challenges and live a happy life for both herself and her daughter.

After years of navigating the parenting journey herself, Freeda knows that sharing her life experiences with others could help them on their own parenting journeys. She has helped countless mothers, fathers, grandparents, babysitters, and teachers in making their lives easier by providing sound advice from her extensive experience with children's behavior patterns over the years.

In her free time, she goes to her Yoga and Pilates classes. She also loves baking, especially when requested by her children. Their favorite is her bunch of chewy white chocolate macadamia cookies.

Check out Freeda's profile on Amazon: https://www.amazon.com/author/freedameighan

Leaving a Review

As an independent author with limited marketing resources, reviews for my books are essential in order to survive as an indie writer. New works of literature get published daily, so there's no guarantee that any given work will be successful.

Your review can help authors like me grow and share their knowledge with more people. If you enjoyed this book, I would really appreciate your honest feedback. You can leave a review by going to this book's page on Amazon, where it is listed, and clicking "Write A Review."

Leaving an honest review can also help other people find this book easily on Amazon and benefit from it as well. Your feedback is important to me so I can find out what you like and don't, which in turn helps me make better decisions about my writing style.

Thank you,

Freeda

References

Bianca Acevedo, Elaine Aron, Sarah Pospos and Dana Jessen, The functional highly sensitive brain: a review of the brain circuits underlying sensory processing sensitivity and seemingly related disorders, Philosophical Transactions of the Royal Society B: Biological Sciences, 10.1098/rstb.2017.0161, 373, 1744, (20170161), (2018).

More Books to Consider

Also available in Audiobook format

LA GUÍA DE LOS PADRES EMPÁTICOS PARA

CRIAR A UN NIÑO MUY SENSIBLE

Estrategias de crianza que aprendí para
entender y alimentar los dones de mi hijo

FREEDA MEIGHAN

LA GUÍA DE LOS PADRES EMPÁTICOS PARA

CRIAR A UN NIÑO ANSIOSO

Cómo ayudar a sus hijos a superar la timidez,
la preocupación, la separación y la ansiedad social

FREEDA MEIGHAN

My good friend, Grace, wrote these books. Please check them out too.

Made in the USA
Monee, IL
10 November 2024

69779993R00052